THREE LETTERS FROM THE COMPANION OF THE BULGARS

St. Rupert of Juvavum

Bishop of Juvavum

Translated by: D.P. Curtin

Dalcassian
Publishing
Company

PHILADELPHIA, PA

ISBN: 978-1-960069-82-5 (Paperback)

Library of Congress Control Number:
Author: Curtin, D.P. (1985-)

Printed by Ingram Content Group, 1 Ingram Blvd, La Vergne, Tennessee

First printing edition 2017.

Introduction

The title and author of this text were initially very mysterious. Fr. Migne had preserved this text in Latin under the title of 'Epistolae Bulgaranus' (Letter of the Bulgars), by a certain 'Comes Bulgaranus' (Count of the Bulgars). The author himself provides a list of kings of Franks of Visigoths, which limits the date of composition to 610-612 AD. This is significant as the Bulgars, as a defined ethnic group, would not be known to history for another twenty years, with the founding of Old Bulgaria, in what is now Ukraine. Ergo, the identification with the Bulgars is an anachronism, likely by a later librarian associating the group of people in question with the later Bulgars. Moreover, no Bulgars are ever mentioned in these letters, which include no subject of address or signature.

It must, therefore, be concluded that these texts were written by someone who dwelt among a Balkan people in the 7th century, bordering their lands on the Frankish frontier. The people who inhabited the eastern Frankish border were the Avars, who held dominion over the regions that would, in a generation's time, become Bulgarian. This would account for the state of confusion over the title. However, its author is then all the more intriguing. The title 'Comes Bulgaranus', which commonly would mean 'Count of the Bulgars', could also be interpreted to mean 'peer' or 'associate' or 'missionary' or 'companion', with the latter two being definitively linked in this time period.

In an attempt to identify the personality who would have lived in the 7th century, inhabited the Frankish frontier, been a Latin churchman, and ministered to the Avar tribes in what would become Bulgaria, we can identify only St. Rupert of Juvavum (Modern Salzberg). His work along the Danube and among the Avar Khanate is well known. However, St. Rupert does appear to be a composite figure, likely composed of at least two men of that name,

'Chrobhertus'. Therefore, these texts represent some of the communication between a Latin missionary in eastern Europe in the early 7th century and a transient Slavic group. They are, therefore, *sui generis*, as most correspondence that survives from this period is in Greek, out of the Imperial capital of Constantinople.

D.P. Curtin
May 31, 2017
Pittsburgh, PA

EPISTLE I

In the meantime, we note to your Holiness that the popular opinion has reached us that Brunigilde the virgin and King Theuderic, under the most bitter disposition, spreading poisons, have incited the king to fight against the glorious King Theutibert, the most atrocious of the barbarians, in the destruction of the united nation. And if this is the case in particular, what is necessary, except that before the weapons of war are drawn up in this part, the divine people should draw up prayers, imploring a vote, whence we ask that the evidence of the matter be made known to us? That we too, who share in the accomplishment of the faithful, rising up with equal fervor of faith, together with all the priests, the clergy, and all the Christian people of this province, may, with litanies, approach the Lord, the Redeemer of all, with supplications. We do this so that he may assert the invincible right hand of his power in the defense of the Catholics, and that he may bring destruction to his treacherous enemy, commensurate with his merits. Let the authors of the quarrels, stripped bare by the ancient serpent's device, be unlocked as an example to all around, asking prostrated by the just vengeance of our Lord. If you have managed to arrange the writings which were sent a little before to the glorious king Theutibert, as you promised, let us know with certainty how that money may be prepared for you. We truly trust that, together with your happiness, we will form a reciprocity of hope with your happy affections.

EPISTLE II

Although the whole axis is seen under the ethereal boundary of the world by the Lord, established by the workman, and by the power of all his mighty men, divided by his wondrous organization, it is necessary that those who guard his evangelical voice, either seek those whom one faith in Christ unites, or love them. However, we may separate ourselves from the temporal dominion of the government, it is fitting that we should not be dissociated from the eternal commandments of the prince. Therefore, we wish to make your happiness flourishing in the heavenly diffusion of grace, and exuberant in spiritual generosity, which the Lord propitiates by the intervening pen, bound by charity, in these letters destined with the utmost desire. Not only do we inquire, but we also teach salvation by addressing the necessary things. Because it is not undeserved that Christ dedicated you as the chief shepherd to his flock, so that with blood-like generosity you may preside over me, most blessed Father, and thus care for the souls of his innumerable sheep. In fact, to persist in such a practice which either greater or less care commits to be employed in peoples, so that in proportion as they are made divine in the most sublime pension, so much should they be unceasingly watchful about those to whom they are placed in existence.

Henceforth, because I do not consider your happiness to be trivial, and as your son Lord Theutibert, with the nation of the Goths, has fallen, as prince can, by the allegation of the experts, has devoted himself to strengthening the perpetual peace through the ambassadors of the same nation. From which he promised to impart to the Franks some thanks due to the merit of money, the number [perhaps, of the Avars] of the nation. Therefore, I am already satisfied that this said son, Lord Theutibert, through your venerable brother Lord and father in Christ, intended for me a true bishop in his writings, by which I know that money has already been directed by your son, my lord King Gundemar. He is here with me, soon to be in Gaul, that he may direct ambassadors prudent from his own sight, and what the entire nation of the Goths hopes for in charity, he promises the traitors that we shall agree with the people. Therefore, I submit your sanctity with due humility, so that as much as you love the Lord Jesus, who leaves the peace of past ages for those to come, you may be pleased to consider this confirmation only for peace. If you acknowledge that the letter which we addressed to the Lord Theutibert has arrived, or if the things which have been entered into under the definition by the ambassadors of the Goths, if they remain truthfully alleged, or as far as your aforesaid son triumphed in the battle of the Abbots [Perhaps, the Avars], we deserve to be informed by your affections.

For it is now known to us, by the opinion of the people, that Queen Brunigilde and King Theuderic, the very Abbots [Perhaps, the Avars], were summoned to fight against the Lord Theutibert, and to migrate from their seats into the province. This was completed so that the utterance of the Catholics is strange to their ears, that under the Christian religion persons are truly far from the Lord established, and they have provoked the Christians to disobey. We do not believe that they exist better than them, but we clearly confirm that the partners who serve from the world of debt crimes are retrieving persons. If, therefore, your sanctity has clearly recognized this, that by the advice of the aforesaid kings, an unholy group has spread itself with hostility over the region of the orthodox prince, you are commanded to declare to us by your pen, that the province belonging to this son of your glorious lord, my lord Gundemar, the king, who has appointed priests with the great people. Let them celebrate the feasts of the fasts so that the hearts of the men who approach unjustly and far from the Lord may be broken by the valor of the warriors, and that the people who guard the dogma of the Christian faith may be commanded by heavenly piety to bestow a trophy.

EPISTLE III.

To the most beloved and most reverend father in Christ, the Bulgarian bishop [Rupert?]. It is known to the Almighty Lord that he is shown to his righteous servant, just as the unjust perishes with the just revenge of damnation. Before these days, I do not think your happiness was hidden away, as the charters of the most glorious kings and the same of your children, Queen Brunigildes and

King Theuderic, were transmitted to us through the same. We should order them by the transmitter himself, and thereafter he announced that the mentioned series of writers, who brought the same writings of their masters together with their own suggestion to us, and that he would receive access to us by writing a supplement to our church books. For with no desire, he chose us neither to search, nor do we need to look at materials from anyone else. We would not have nodded if he had come to announce the answer of his lords, only because he had not hastened, for he was the most wicked of your men, whose approach to the presence of your glorious son Lord Gundemar, the king was to be lamented. Let it shine forth, with all justice which you see in the inner mirror, disguised by the unjust excuses of mere words. Who does not look forward to your sanctity, and to those whom you have aggravated by unlawful acts, with the parcels of flattering speeches intended to soften them? For we consider such a dissimulation of yours, if you grant me pardon. Such as if every debtor, lifted up by human shame, by the incitement of impudence, strikes the moneylender with prerogatives, and the humble creditor conceals the truth, which the slanderer utterly shames by speaking.

For there remains to your glorious son, my lord Gundemar the king, and to the whole nation of the Goths, not a little but a great reparation of money, as your noble ambassadors of the same nation, running most magnificently with the comfort of the grace of truth, were captured by your unjust prince. With the double generosity of malice, let them bear the shame of all relegation and the shame of want. Let it be known, indeed, that the illustrious men of Toledo and Gundrimir, directed by my most serene lord King Gundemar, in your borders to the place of the Irapinas, after the insult they had inflicted upon them, shut them up among the precepts, and denied access even to you in a rich manner. Behold, what part you have committed to your own lot is not unknown to your minds. So much as the bitterness from your injury, in addition to the bitterness of your ambassadors to the presence of my illustrious lord, you complain of opening the way by feigning letters. Let the highest prince from the heavenly throne see this cause. Let the divine part stab with vengeance who has unjustly been seen to cause trouble to the part of another, and who, by rejecting charity, has violated the peace of the highest power, which he has cunningly loved.

Although I had received the same letters from the sons of the kings as well as yours, I immediately reformed their written record, which if the mentioned glorious princes had received, or whether it had been brought to your knowledge, we found no denunciation. We ,therefore, also declare your honors, if you desire to keep the peace in a type removed from pretense, which is known to be the greatest lot of dominion, and agree to love Christ with the Goths with a heart adapted to remain devoted. It is not necessary that they should be uttered only by false lips, but that the peace which they themselves first rushed upon us, by perfect works, should be demonstrated. It is worthy of you that the ambassadors of the Goths be restored to their dignity as soon as possible. That is, between a nation of kindred blood keeping peace, with the Lord's adjutant, let your legates, if necessary, remain free to travel to the presence of my glorious lord. For the places from which you intimated Jubinianus and Cornelianus, which in the province of the Goths are known to have been possessed by the ladies Brunigildes, so that we may give access to their people after his right.

We marvel at your blessedness to order us to encourage us in this way, so that the places which, for the stability of the concord of holy memory, our lord Recharedus the king, in the law mentioned, contradicted the ladies (so that the covenant of charity may be broken by your parties who nurture scandal) of the Goths. For I think that what your party is known to have admitted unjustly, if you choose to make amends, will be able to unite your nation in charity, and defend the same places as Lady Brunigildes holds by right. Since we remember you, most blessed man, until now with kind hearts and ageless pursuits, and too much to fear the Almighty. How can you care if the charity of both unharmed agents has been dedicated to God so many times by princes? So that the peace which was once brought together by the former nations of both nations, now remains dissolved, while it ought to have been strengthened forever by your counsel?

LATIN TEXT

EPISTOLA I

. . . . . Interea notescimus sanctitati vestrae ad nos opinione vulgata pervenisse Brunigildem virginem et Theudericum regem amarissima sub dispositione assueta diffundentes venena, in excidium unitae gentis contra gloriosum Theutibertum regem atrocissimum barbarorum excitasse dimicare regem. Quod si specialiter ita res agitur, quid necesse est, nisi ut ante arma bellica cunctus in hac parte precibus elaboret divinum populus implorando suffragium, unde petimus evidentiam rei nobis significari? Ut et nos participes effecti fidelium pari fidei flagrantia consurgentes, cum universis sacerdotibus, clero, cunctaque hujus provinciae Christianorum plebe, indictis letaniis redemptorem omnium Dominum supplicationibus adeamus; ut invictam potentiae suae in defensione catholicorum praetendat dexteram, et aemulan tis perfidi hostis condignum meritis adsit intentionis interitum; atque jurgiorum auctores, vetusti serpentis machinatione nudatos in exemplum reserata clareat cunctis per circuitu justa nostri Domini ultione prostratos poscentes. Ut si scripta quae paulo ante glorioso Theutiberto regi directa, sicut polliciti estis, destinare procurastis: aut si missi vestri jam reversi sunt, vel quod reciperetis responsum, vel si usque hic placita deportantes, aut certe si ad praesentiam gloriosissimi domini mei Gundemari regii praeparaturi advenerint, certius sciamus Quomodo aut tibi pecunia praeparetur, nos veraciter ut confidimus una cum beatitudine vestra sospitatem reciprocatis formare jubeatis affectibus.

EPISTOLA II

Etsi universus axe sub aethereo limes terrarum Domino cernitur opifice constitutus, et omnium potestate pollentium ipsius mirabile constet ordinatione divisus, necesse est ut ejus evangelicam vocem custodientes, vel quaerere eos quos una in Christum fides consociat, vel diligere; et quamlibet a temporali dominatione segregemur imperii, congruet ut praeceptis principis non dissociemur aeterni. Unde beatitudinem vestram gratia coelesti diffusione florentem, et spirituali largitione exuberantem quam Domino propitiante intercurrente stylo effici volumus charitate devinctum, his destinatis cum summo desiderio litteris; non solum inquirimus, sed et salutis cum debito necessariarum rerum alloquio impertimus. Quia non immerito praecipuum te pastorem suo Christus dedicavit ovili, ut cum velut sanguinis generositate mihi, beatissime Pater, praepolleas, ita de suarum innumeras ovium geras sollicitudinem animarum. Tali quippe in usu persistere quibus vel major vel minor cura in populis adhibenda committit: ut quantum divina efficiuntur in pensione sublimiores, tantum debent circa his quibus praeponuntur existere indesinenter pervigiles. Et quia latere beatitudinem vestram non arbitror quod filius vester dominus Theutibertus cum gente Gothorum a decidentibus velut olim existit colligata principibus, nunc per peritorum allegatione pacem per legatis ejusdem gentis devovit roborare perpetuam. Ex quo aliquod gratiae merito pecuniae, numerum [Forte, Avarorum] gentis pollicitus est impertire Francorum. Unde jam me constat, memorato filio vestro domino Theutiberto per venerabilem fratrem vestrum dominum et in Christo mihi patrem verum episcopum destinasse scripta, per quas innotui quod jam pecunia a filio vestro domno meo Gundemaro rege directa. Hic mihi in Gallias esse dignoscitur, ut prudentes ex suo dirigat conspectu legatos: et ea quae ob charitatem gens Gothorum sperat universa, promittit tradentibus placita saltem contradamus hominibus. Obinde tuam sanctitatem debita humilitate deposco, ut quantum Dominum diligis Jesum, qui pacem praeteritis saeculis dereliquit futuris, hujus confirmatione pro pacis tantum intendere digneris delectabiliter. Et si agnoscitis eam quam direximus ad domnum Theutibertum paginam pervenisse; aut si ea quae per legatis Gothorum sunt sub definitione inita, si manebunt veraciter allegata, vel quantum praedictus filius vester in Abatorum [Forte, Avarorum] bellica triumphatus est acie, vestris mereamur affectibus informari. Nam et nobis currenti est opinione plebis compertum, quod Brunigildes reginae et Theuderici regis ipsos Abates [Forte, Avares] ad bellandum domni Theutiberti convocatos et de suis sedibus transmigrare provinciam: quod enuntiare catholicorum infandum est auribus, ut Christiana sub religione personas revera procul a Domino constitutas, in Christianorum provocarent desaevire. Nec credimus eos ab illis existere meliores, sed ita manifeste socios comprobamus qui de mundum debitis scelerum ministrat retamenta personas. Hoc igitur vestra sanctitas si evidenter agnovit, quod ex praedictorum regum consilio super orthodoxi principis regionem impia se fudit hostilitate caterva, per vestro nobis declarare jubeatis stylo, ut hac filii vestri gloriosi domini mei Gundemari regis ad ordinationem nostram pertinente provincia, indicta sacerdotes cum populo omnipotenti celebrent jejuniorum solemnia; ut accedentium injuste atque longe a domino corda virorum, siderea confringat virtute bellantium, et gente Christianae fidei dogma custodienti laudabilem coelesti pietate jubeatis conferre tropaeum

EPISTOLA III.

Dilectissimo atque in Christo reverendissimo Patri episcopo Bulgaranus.. . . . Notum est Domino omnipotenti qui justum indicat servum, et injustum justa damnationis ultione perimet, quia ante hos dies, quod tuam non reor latuisse beatitudinem, chartas gloriosissimorum regum idemque filiorum vestrorum Brunigildes reginae et Theuderici regis, per eodem nobis fuere transmissas. Et ut eas ipso praeciperemus tradente, memoratorum series scriptorum denuntiavisse, qui eadem suorum scripta dominorum una cum suam ad nos usque suggestionem deduxi, et ut aditum ad nos perciperet commeandi supplex scribendo nostram ordinationem poscit. Nam nullo cum desiderio, neque exquirere elegit nos, neque ab nullis indigimus intueri materiis; et quam neque si venisset pro responso dominorum suorum denuntiando annueramus: tantum quia minime properavit, nequissimus nam de homine vestrum illum cujus ad praesentiam filii vestri gloriosi domini Gundemari regis efflagitare videmini aditum, debet mens vestra in summo propositionis tabescere exordio, dum veritas vobis experto lumine fulgeat, et justitiam quam speculo interiori prospicitis, injusta verborum excusatione dissimuletis. Quis vestrae non prospiciat sanctitatis ingenium, et ea quae actibus exasperastis illicitis, blandis intenditis eloquiorum lenire tendiculis? Talem enim vestram, si veniam tribuitis, dissimulationem censemus. Quale si quisque debitor humano pudore sublato, proterviae incitamento, praerogativis feneratorem pulset objectionibus et veritatem habeus pusilentus creditor tegat, quam calumniator loquendo penitus erubescat. Manet enim filio vestro glorioso domno meo Gundemaro regi cunctaeque genti Gothorum non exigua sed magna pecuniae repetitio, ut nobiles ejusdem gentis legatos vestra magnificentissime cum consolato veritatis gratia discurrentes ab vestro injuste principe capti. Geminata malitiae largitate dedecus omne relegationis perferant egestatis opprobrio. Pateat vero Totilanem et Gundrimirum viros illustres a serenissimo domino meo Gundemaro rege directos, in finibus vestris in locum Irapinas post illatam eorum despectionem inter praeceptione clausistis, et ad vos usque succedere loculenter aditum denegastis. Ecce quae pars vestra commiserit vestris non sunt incognita mentibus; et tantum a vobis injuriae acerbitatem vehentibus insuper vestrorum ad praesentia inclyti domini mei legatorum, vestri simulando litteris, viam aperire conqueritis. Videat altissimus a coelesti solio princeps hanc causam; et divina partem ultione confodiat qui injuste parti alterius visus est conferre molestiam, et qui charitatem respuendo pacem excelsae potestatis violaverit captiose dilectam. Licet dum filiorum regum idemque vestrorum litteras accepissem, eorum protinus reformavi rescriptum quod si memorati gloriosi principes acceperunt, sive in vestra fuerit cognitione deductum, nullo denuntiante comperimus. Sed et vestrae itaque honorificentiae declaramus, si remoto simulationis pacem typo servare desideratis, quae dominio maxima sors esse cognoscitur, et Christum diligenda concordes cum Gothis corde aptatis permanere devoto; non oportet ut ea tantum labiis fallentibus proferatis, sed pacem quam nobis servantibus ipsi prius irruere, perfectis demonstrandum operibus demonstretis. Dignum est vestri ut primum in sua dignitate Gothorum restituantur legati; et inter affinem sanguinis gentem servantem pacem, Domino adjuvante, vestrorum, si necesse est, ad praesentiam gloriosi domini mei libertas maneat itineris legatorum. Nam de locis unde intimastis Jubiniano et Corneliano, quae in provincia Gothorum noscitur domna Brunigildes possedisse, ut suis post ejus jure aditum tribuamus hominibus; ordinandam miramur tuam sic nos hortare beatitudinem, ut loca quae pro stabilitate concordiae sanctae memoriae dominus noster Recharedus rex in jure memoratae contradidit domnae (ut) a partibus vestris scandalum nutrientibus foedus sit charitatis disruptum: et pars jura quae stimulum illicite suscitat, jura debeat gentis possidere Gothorum. Arbitror enim ut ea quae pars vestra injuste noscitur admisisse, si emendare malueritis, poterit gentem vestramque in charitate connexam, eadem suo jure domna Brunigildes defendere loca. Te quippe, beatissime vir, dum hactenus benignis animis, et saecularibus evigilantem studiis, nimisque formidare omnipotentem meminimus? Quomodo cures si tantis temporibus charitas utriusque illaesa agentis es Deo dicatus antistes a principibus, ut quae pax olim a prioribus gentium utrarum gentibus colligata, nunc maneat dissoluta, dum vestro debuit ex consilio in perpetuum existere roborata?

The Scriptorium Project is the work of a small group of lay people of various apostolic churches who are interested in the preservation, transmission, and translation of the works of the early and medieval church. Our efforts are to make the works of the church fathers accessible to anyone who might have an interest in Christian antiquities and the theological, philosophical, and moral writings that have become the bedrock of Western Civilization.

To-date, our releases have pulled from the Greek, Syriac, Georgian, Latin, Celtic, Ethiopian, and Coptic traditions of Christianity, and have been pulled from sundry local traditions and languages.

Other Titles and Translations by D.P. Curtin:

Lebor Gabala Erenn by Nennius the Monk (2017)
The Eight Vices by Eutropis of Valencia (2017)
Three Letters from the Companion of the Bulgars by St. Rupert of Juvavum (2017)
Privileges of the Abbot of Canterbury by St. Augustine of Canterbury (2017)
Nicene Canons in the Old Nubian Language (2018)
Apology to Gunthamund, King of Vandals by Aemeilius Dracontius (2018)
First Book of Ethiopian Maccabees (2018)
Chronicon: a short chronicle of Visigothic Spain by Eutrandus of Ticino (2019)
Decrees of Aethelbert by St. Aethelbert, King of Kent (2019)
The Measure to be taxed for Penance by St. Columba of Iona (2019)
Protoevangelium of James: Greek and English Texts (2019)
Edicts of the Synod of Paris by Chlothar II, King of Franks (2019)
The Life of St. Desiderius by Sisebut, King of Visigoths (2019)
The Synod of Rome by St. Boniface IV of Rome (2019)
Letter to Pope Theodore by Victor of Carthage (2020)
The Decree of 610 by Gundemar, King of Visigoths (2020)
Laws of the Church by Chlothar III, King of Franks (2020)
Donations by St. Aethelbert, King of Kent (2020)
The Mystical Interpretation by St. Aileran the Wise (2020)
Laws of the Church by St. Dagobert II, King of Franks (2020)
The Old Nubian Miracle of St. Mena (2021)
About Fifteen Problems by St. Albertus Magnus (2022)
Testament of Some Former Things by John Scotus Eriugena (2022)
The Georgian Synaxarium (2022)
Instructions: Counsel for Novices by St. Ammonas the Hermit (2022)
The Syriac Menologium and Martyrology (2022)
Book on Religious Exercise and Quiet by St. Isaiah the Solitary (2022)
Vision of Theophilus by St. Cyril of Alexandria (2022)
On Fate (De Fato) by St. Albertus Magnus (2023)
Fragments of 'Chronicle' by Hippolytus of Thebes (2023)
Life of the Blessed Theotokos by Epiphanius Monachus (2023)
Syriac Life of John the Baptist by Serapion the Presbyter (2023)
Second Book of Ethiopian Maccabees (2023)